Guidance

How to use this book:

This workbook contains over 100 questions specifically designed to advc
money knowledge.
Our years of experience have enabled us to put together the perfect balance of fluency,
reasoning questions and vocabulary checks.

Each page is dedicated to one of the current curriculum objectives.

You will find pages of fluency questions. These questions help develop maths concepts quickly and you will see various questions framed in different ways in order for your child to secure their understanding of the objective. This means your child will not just be memorising facts, but have a real conceptual understanding.

There will then be a page of reasoning questions.
Reasoning will allow your child to explore these objectives at a deeper level and show if your child has truly mastered these concepts.
It requires children to use mathematical vocabulary, explore trial and error and explain how they have reached their answers.

There will be a space for your child to write their answers down.
If your child prefers to explain this verbally, this is equally acceptable.

There is a great assessment tool at the back to check your child's progress and identify any gaps in your child's knowledge. If you find that there are any gaps in their knowledge- visit our website- www.masterthecurriculum.co.uk for plenty of free resources!

Our books feature in the monthly maths subscription box: maths minds. To find out more, visit mathsminds.co.uk

These workbooks are dedicated to Tia, Leanna and Malachi.

Contents

Money

Coins and notes used to pay for items.

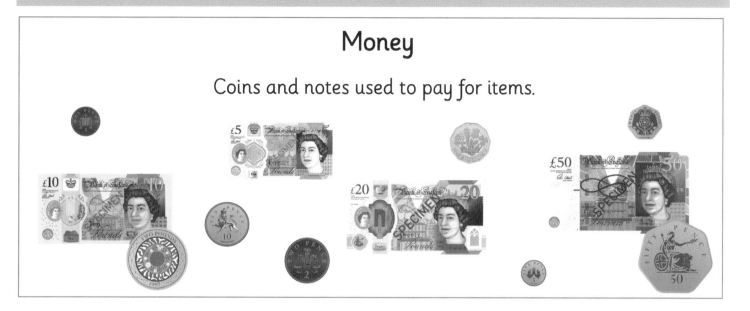

Pence

Pence is used in the U.K. 100 pence equals one pound.

The letter p is used to represent pence.

| 1p | 2p | 5p | 10p | 20p | 50p |

Pounds

The symbol used for pounds is £.
We use pounds in the U.K.
There are 100 pence in a pound.

Fifty pounds
£50

One pound
£1

Coins

Coins are small and metal.
Most of our coins are round.

All the pence are coins.
Some of the pounds are coins.

Notes

There are 4 banknotes in the U.K.
They used to be made from paper.

Now they are made from a material called polymer.

Measurement: Money
Recognise and use symbols for pounds and pence

Label the money. Use the symbol for pounds and pence correctly.

A)

B)
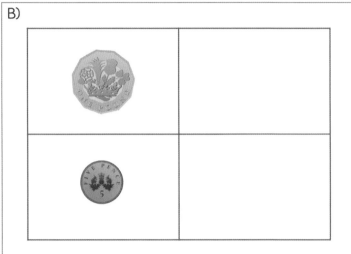

C)

D)

E)
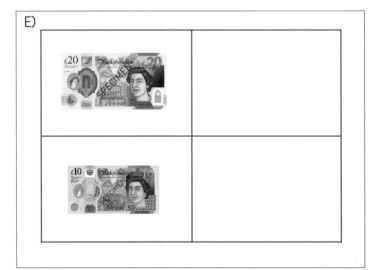

F)
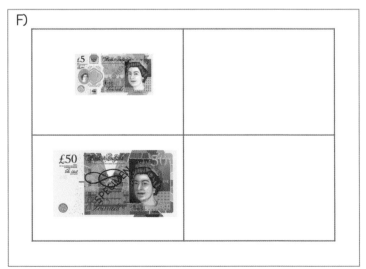

Measurement: Money

Understand the value of coins: Counting

Shade in the coins to show how much the ice cream is worth.

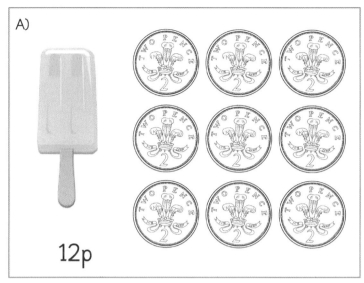

A)

12p

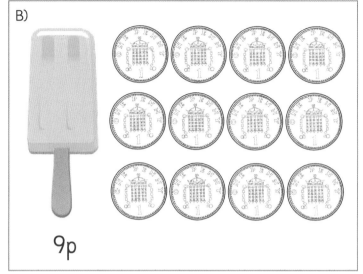

B)

9p

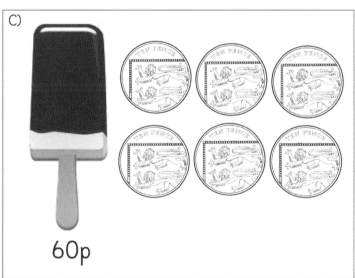

C)

60p

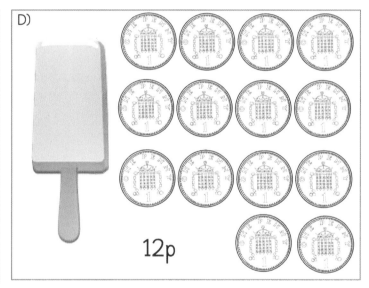

D)

12p

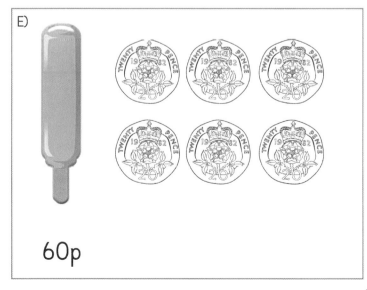

E)

60p

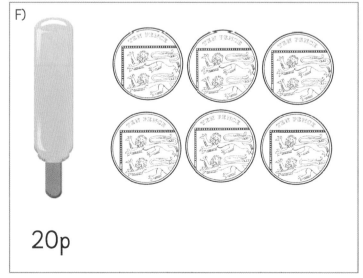

F)

20p

Measurement: Money

Count totals of money using pence

How much does each ice-cream cost?

A) _____p

B) _____p

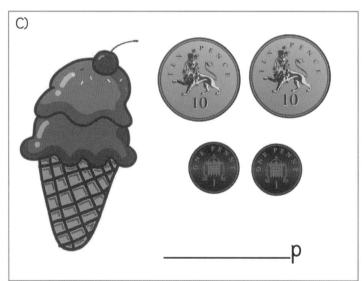

C) _____p

D) _____p

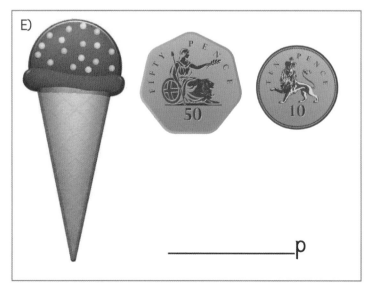

E) _____p

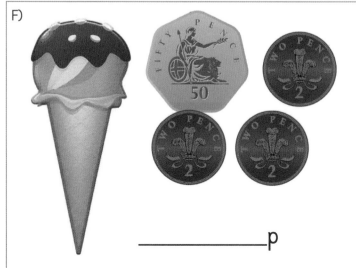

F) _____p

Measurement: Money

Count totals of money using pounds

How much does each ice-cream cost?

A)

£_____

B)

£_____

C)

£_____

D)

£_____

E)

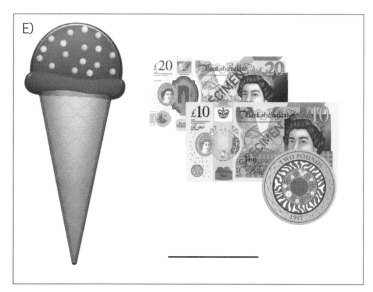

_____

F)

_____

Measurement: Money

Count totals of money using pence *or* pounds

How much money is there altogether? Remember to write the symbol for pence or pounds.

A)

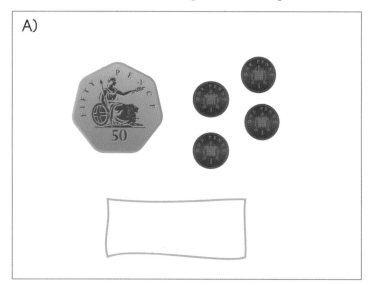

B)

C)

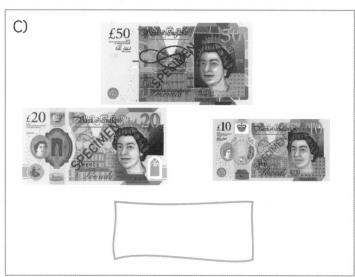

D)

E)

F)

Measurement: Money

Count totals of money using pence *or* pounds

Count your pounds and pence to find out how much is in each piggy bank or wallet.

G)

£_____

H)

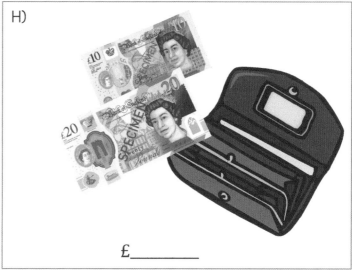

£_____

I)

_____p

J)

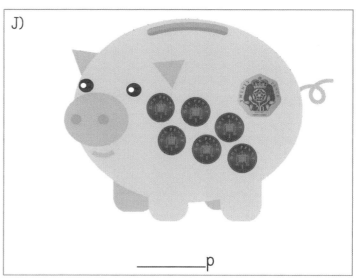

_____p

K)

£_____

L)

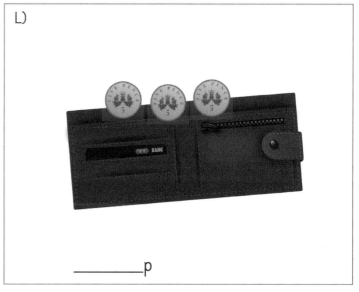

_____p

7.

1. What mistake has Rosie made?

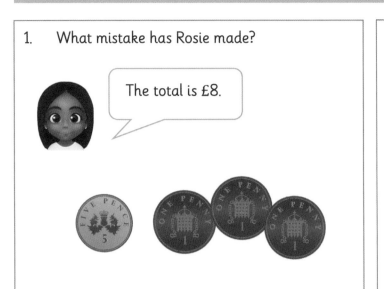

The total is £8.

Explain or prove your answers here.

2. What do you think about the conversation?

Malachi

I have two silver coins that total £1.

Esin

That's impossible!

Explain or prove your answers here.

3. Which is the odd one out? Why?

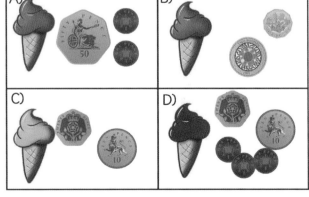

Explain or prove your answers here.

Measurement: Money
Combine amounts to make a particular value

A) Circle the coins I need to make 3 pence.

B) Circle the coins I need to make 4 pence.

C) Circle the coins or notes I need to make £6.

D) Circle the coins or notes I need to make £7.

E) Circle the coins I need to make 2 pence.

F) Circle the coins or notes I need to make 6 pence.

Measurement: Money

Combine amounts to make a particular value

Circle the money you need to pay for the aliens.

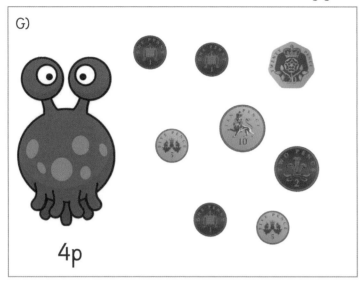

G) 4p

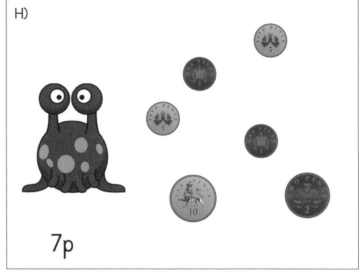

H) 7p

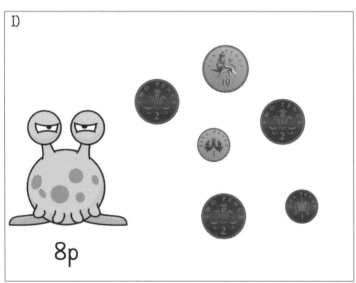

I) 8p

J) £8

K) £9

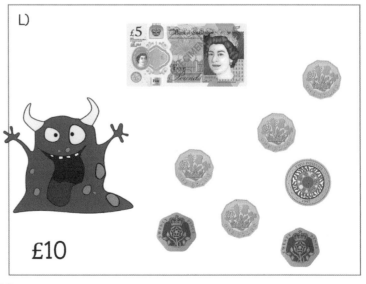

L) £10

Measurement: Money
Combine amounts to make a particular value

What coins will you use to make the given value? Circle them.

M)

28p

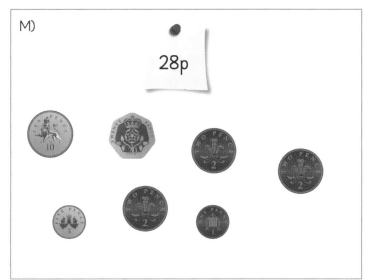

N)

40p

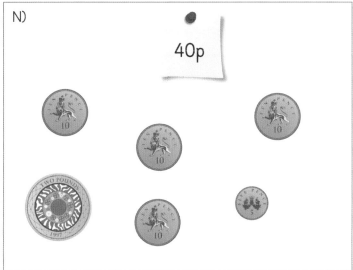

O)

35p

P)

59p

Q)

77p

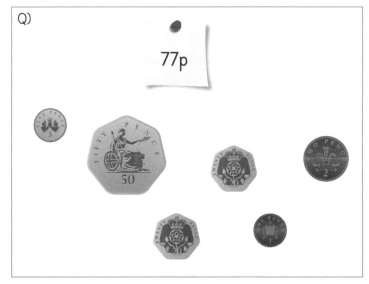

R)

83p

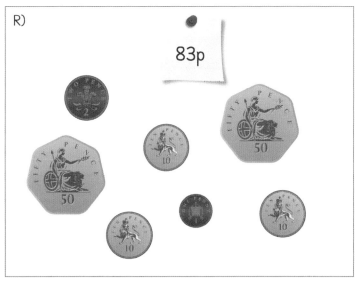

Measurement: Money
Combine amounts to make a particular value

Look at the ice-creams. What coins would you use to make the amounts? Draw them.

A)

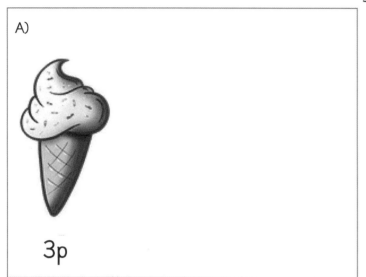

3p

B)

4p

C)

7p

D)

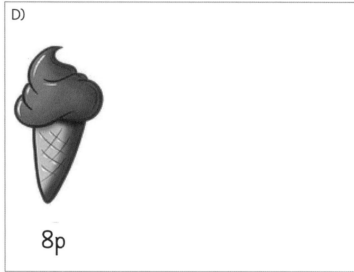

8p

E)

9p

F)

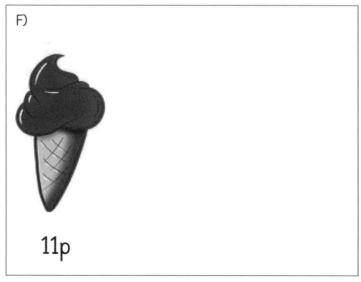

11p

1. Leanna is making a value.
   What value is she making?

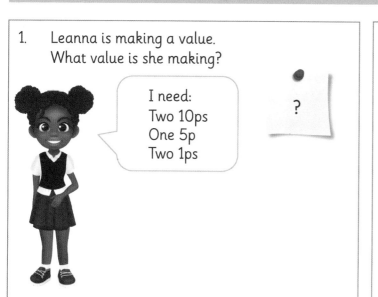

I need:
Two 10ps
One 5p
Two 1ps

?

Explain or prove your answers here.

2. Zach's jar has 18p in it. Which jar is Zach's?

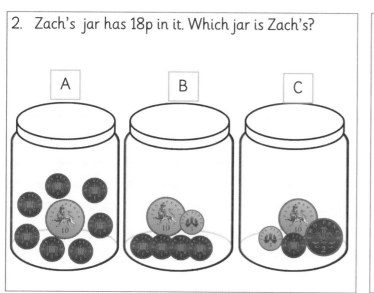

A   B   C

Explain or prove your answers here.

3. True or False?

You can make 60p with 3 coins.

Explain or prove your answers here.

Measurement: Money

Find different combinations of coins that equal the same amount of money

Circle the items that are worth the same amount.

A)

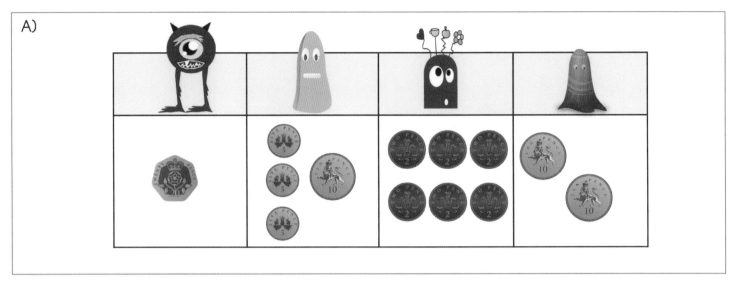

B)

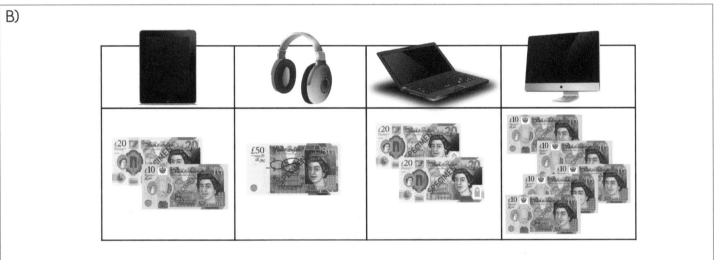

C)

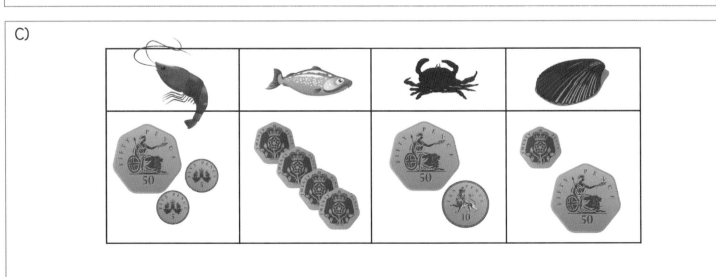

Measurement: Money

Find different combinations of coins that equal the same amount of money

Find 4 different ways to make these amounts. Draw circles for the coins.

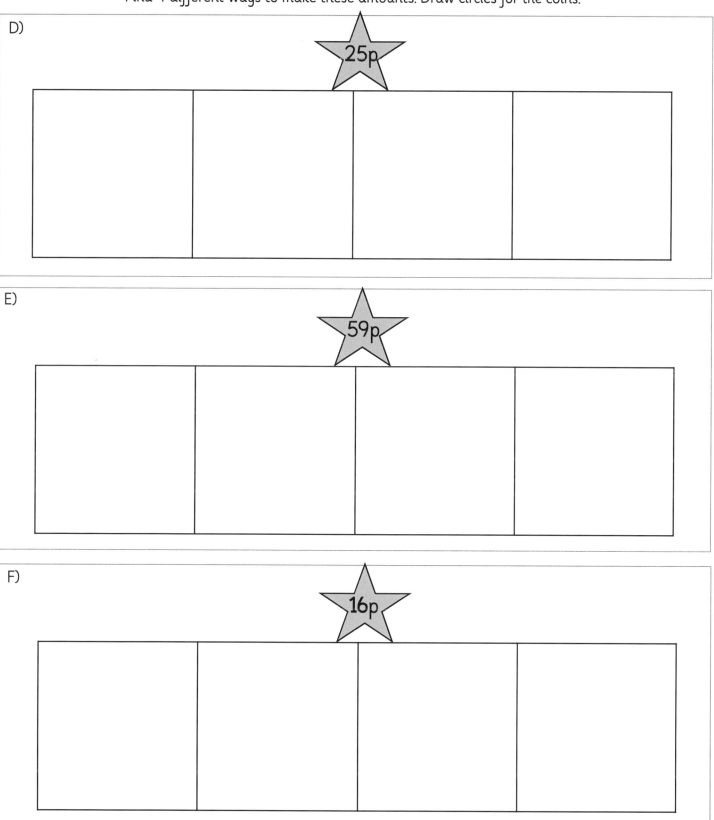

D) 25p

E) 59p

F) 16p

Measurement: Money
Find different combinations of coins that equal the same amount of money

Find 4 different ways to make these amounts. Draw circles for coins and rectangles for notes.

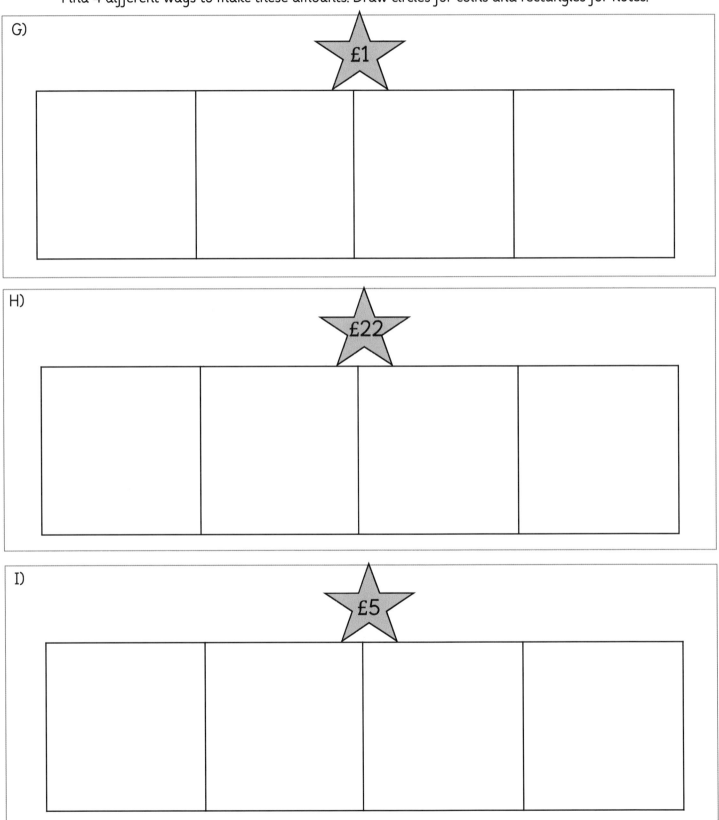

G) ★ £1

H) ★ £22

I) ★ £5

Measurement: Money

Add amounts of money, using £ or p

Look at the items I have bought. How much was spent altogether?

A)

_____ p

B)

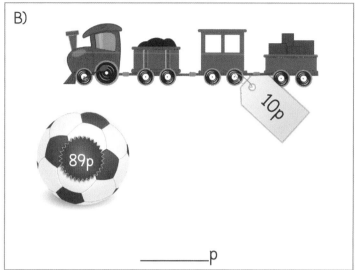

_____ p

C)

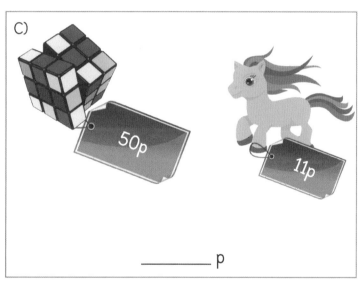

_____ p

D)

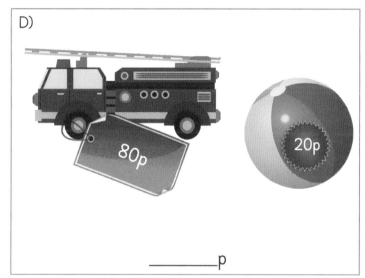

_____ p

E)

_____ p

F)

_____ p

Measurement: Money
Working out change from 10p

I buy these items with this coin: How much change will I receive?

A)

9 p

Change:

B)

6 p

Change:

C)

10 p

Change:

D)

5 p

Change:

E)

1 p

Change:

F)

4 p

Change:

G)

2 p

Change:

H)

3 p

Change:

I)

3 p + 5 p

Change:

J)

8 p + 2 p

Change:

Measurement: Money
Working out change from 20p

I buy these items with this coin: How much change will I receive?

A)

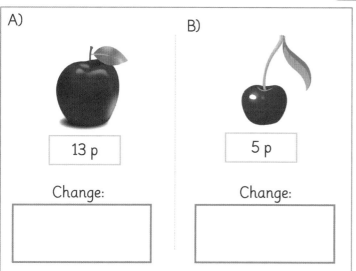

13 p	5 p

B)

Change:

Change:

C)

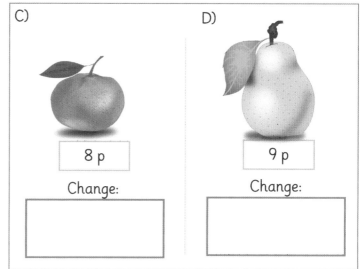

8 p	9 p

D)

Change:

Change:

E)

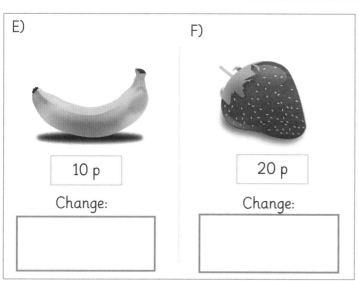

10 p	20 p

F)

Change:

Change:

G)

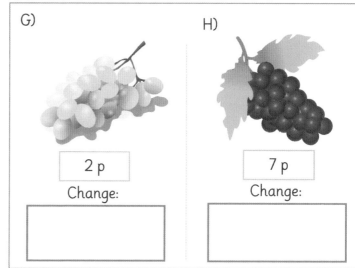

2 p	7 p

H)

Change:

Change:

I)

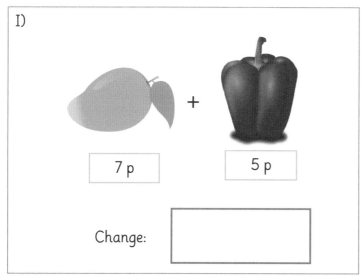

7 p	+	5 p

Change:

J)

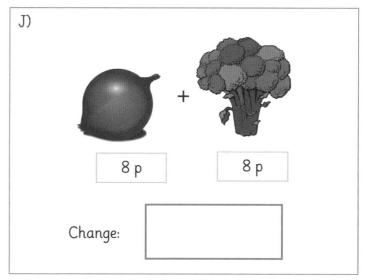

8 p	+	8 p

Change:

Measurement: Money
Working out change from 50p

I buy these items with this coin: 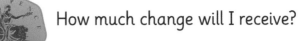 How much change will I receive?

A)

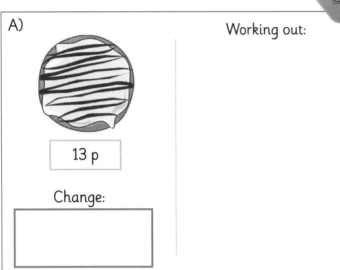

13 p

Working out:

Change:

B)

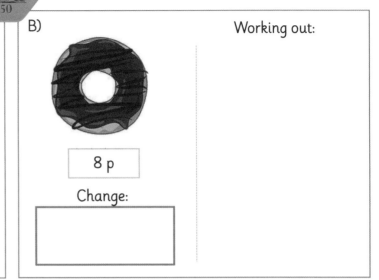

8 p

Working out:

Change:

C)

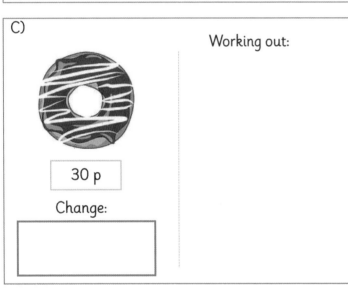

30 p

Working out:

Change:

D)

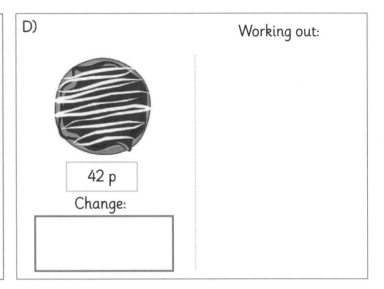

42 p

Working out:

Change:

E)

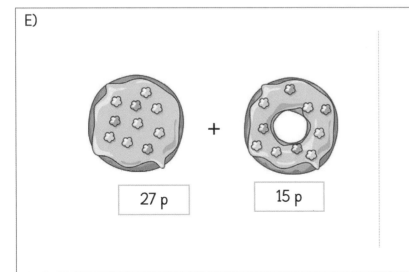

27 p + 15 p

Working out:

Change:

20.

Measurement: Money
Working out change

---

1. Always, Sometimes, Never?

When you buy an item, you will always receive change.

Explain or prove your answers here.

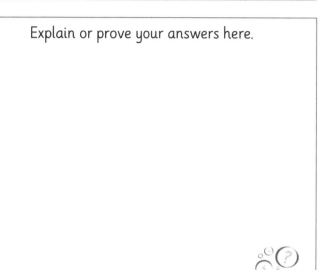

---

2. Both children pay 25p.
Who will receive the most change?

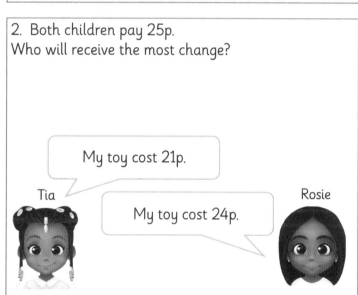

Tia — My toy cost 21p.

My toy cost 24p. — Rosie

Explain or prove your answers here.

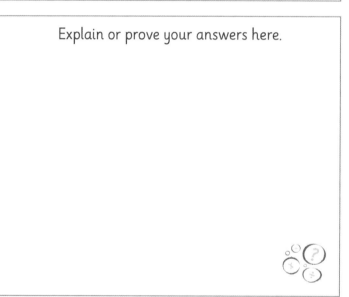

---

3. I bought 2 items with a 20p coin and received 5p change.
What items did I buy?

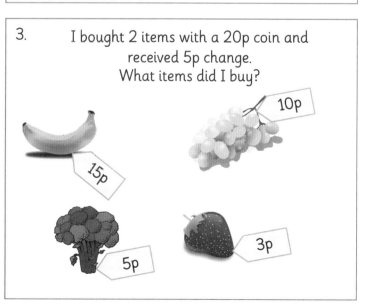

10p

15p

5p

3p

Explain or prove your answers here.

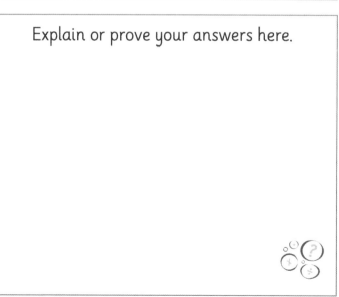

Money Assessment

Colour in the smiley face to show your understanding of the objectives.

 I understand this well.

 I understand some parts.

 I would like more help.

Recognise all coins and notes	☺
Understand the value of each coin (counting)	☺
Count totals of money using pounds or pence	☺
Combine amounts to make a particular value	☺
Find different combinations of coins that equal the same amount of money	☺
Add amounts of money	☺
Work out change	☺

Do you know what these words mean? Tick the words that you know.
Go back to the beginning to revise the words you do not know.

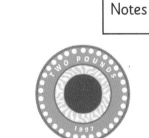

Money	
Pence	
Pounds	
Coins	
Notes	

Answers

Page 2: Recognise and use symbols for pounds and pence

A) 1p, 10p   B) £1, 5p   C) 2p, £2   D) 20p, 50p   E) £20, £10   F) £5, £50

Page 3: Recognise coins and notes

A) 6 coins shaded   B) 9 coins shaded   C) 6 coins shaded   D) 12 coins shaded   E) 3 coins shaded   F) 2 coins shaded

Page 4: Count totals of money using pence

A) 9p   B) 11p   C) 22p   D) 24p   E) 60p   F) 56p

Page 5: Count totals of money using pounds

A) £3   B) £5   C) £12   D) £11   E) £32   F) £9

Page 6 - 8: Count totals of money using pounds or pence

A) 54p   B) £7   C) £80   D) 37p   E) 100p/ £1   F) 100p/ £1   G) £12   H) £30   I) 8p   J) 26p   K) £25   L) 15p

Reasoning
1.   Rosie has counted in pounds instead of pence
2.   Esin is wrong, it is possible if Malachi has 2 fifty pence pieces.
3.   Possible answers: A- the only one which doesn't contain a 3; B, the only one with pound coins

Page 9 - 11 : Understand the value of coins: Counting

A) 2p and 1p   B) 2p + 2p   C) £5 and £1   D) £5 + £2 OR £5, £1 and £1   E) 1p + 1p   F) 5p + 1p
G) 2p, 1p and 1p   H) 5p and 2p OR 5p, 1p and 1p   I) 5p, 2p and 1p.   J) £5, £2 and £1
K) £5, £2, £1, £1 or £5, £1, £1, £1, £1,   L) £5, £2, £1, £1, £1   M)20p, 5p, 2p, 1p   N) 10p, 10p, 10p, 10p
O) 20p, 10p, 2p, 2p, 1p   P) 50p, 5p, 2p, 1p, 1p   Q)50p, 20p, 5p, 2p   R) 50p, 10p, 10p, 10p, 2p, 1p

Page 12 - 13 : Combine amounts to make a particular value (drawing coins)

A) 2p and 1p/ 1p x 3   B) 2p + 2p / 1p x 4/ 2p, 1p, 1p   C) 5p and 2p / 5p, 1p, 1p / 1p x 7
D) 5p, 2p, 1p/ 2p x 4/ 1p x 8 / 5p and 1p x 3   E) 1p x 9 / 5p and 1p x 4 / 5p, 2p, 2p / 2p x 4 and 1p
F) 10p + 1p / 1p x 11 / 5p, 5p and 1p

Reasoning
1. 27p
2. Jar C
3. True. 20p, 20p and 20p

Answers

Page 14: Find different combinations of coins that equal the same amount of money

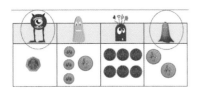  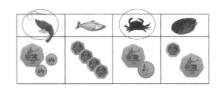

Page 15 - 16: Find different combinations of coins that equal the same amount of money: Drawing coins (Examples)

Example answers:
D) 25p / 20p + 5p / 10p + 10p + 5p / 5p + 5p + 5p + 5p + 5p
E) 50p + 5p + 2p + 2p / 50p + 5p + 2p + 1p + 1p / 50p + 5p + 1p + 1p + 1p + 1p / 20p + 20p + 10p + 5p + 2p + 2p
F) 10p + 5p + 1p / 10p + 2p + 2p + 2p / 5p + 5p + 5p + 1p / 5p + 5p + 2p + 2p + 2p
G) £1 / 50p + 50p / 50p + 20p + 20p + 10p / 50p + 20p + 20p + 5p + 5p
H) £20 + £2 / £20 + £1 + £1 / £10 + £10 + £2 / £10 + £10 + £1 + £1
I) £5 / £2 + £2 + £1 / £2 + £2 + 50p + 50p / £2 + £1 + £1 + 50p + 50p

Page 17: Add amounts of money using £ or p

A) 66p   B) 99p   C) 61p   D) 100p / £1   E) 65p   F) 68p

Page 18: Working out change from 10p

A) 1p   B) 4p   C) 0p   D) 5p   E) 9p   F) 6p   G) 8p   H) 7p   I)2p   J) 0p

Page 19: Working out change from 20p

A) 1p   B) 4p   C) 0p   D) 5p   E) 9p   F) 6p   G) 8p   H) 7p   I)2p   J) 0p

Page 20 - 21 : Working out change from 50p

A) 37p   B) 42p   C) 20p   D) 8p   E) 8p

Reasoning
1. Sometimes. It depends if your item is worth less than what you have paid. You will then receive change.
2. Tia will because her item is worth less than Rosie's.
3. Grapes and broccoli

Printed in Great Britain
by Amazon